BABY ANIMALS

Kittens

Kate Petty

BARRON'S

Mother and babies

A mother cat is pregnant for nine weeks. She looks quite fat and you can sometimes see the kittens moving around inside her. When she is ready to have the kittens the mother settles down in a quiet place. As each tiny kitten is born she licks it clean. There are usually four or five kittens in a litter.

A pregnant cat is as agile as ever.

This sleeping kitten is four days old. ▷

First days

The eyes and ears of newborn kittens are closed, but somehow they manage to find their way to one of their mother's teats. Soon they are happily drinking milk. Very young kittens spend most of their time suckling and sleeping. The mother cat seems contented with her babies and purrs when she is feeding them.

A large litter of kittens drinking milk from their mother.

Sleeping kittens ▷

A closer look

The week-old kitten is twice the size of the newborn. Its tiny ears are still folded and its eyes have only just opened. It cannot yet make sense of what it sees. A kitten's eyes are usually gray-blue at first. They start to change color at around five weeks, eventually turning green or gold. Some breeds of cats have unusual blue eyes all their lives.

This kitten's eyes have changed color.

Tabby kitten at one week old ▷

First steps

By three weeks a kitten's legs are strong enough for it to stagger around. If the mother wants to move a kitten in a hurry she will pick it up with her mouth. By four weeks kittens are quite steady on their feet. Now they start to run and jump. The mother will still watch out for them though, and will carry them back in her mouth if they stray too far.

The mother carries the kitten painlessly by the scruff of its neck.

This kitten is four weeks old. ▷

Washing

Cats spend a lot of time washing and grooming themselves. The mother cat washes her kittens very thoroughly with her rough tongue, holding them down with a firm paw if they try to wriggle away. The little kittens quickly copy her and learn to lick their paws and wash all over, even behind the ears.

Kittens washing themselves

This kitten has no chance of escape. ▷

Mealtime

Kittens drink milk from their mother until they are about eight weeks old. At about four weeks they can try solid food and learn to lap milk from a saucer. Pet kittens need to eat several small meals a day. They will usually curl up to sleep after they have eaten. Kittens will drink water occasionally too so there should always be some left for them.

Kittens soon drink from a saucer or dish.

Even the smallest kittens growl when they eat meat. ▷

Playtime

Kittens are very playful creatures. As they play they are learning as well. All cats are hunters and kittens need to practice their hunting skills before they try to catch a meal on the move. The mother cat sometimes joins in their play, swishing her tail from side to side so that the kittens can pounce on it.

Kittens need to be able to pounce if they are going to catch mice.

Looking for something to pounce on in the straw ▷

Mischief

A kitten's playfulness can often lead it into mischief. A pet kitten has to learn that it is fine to run up a tree trunk but not up the curtains. Or that it can play with a piece of string but not with the dangling corner of a tablecloth. Kittens soon calm down as they get older, although even adult cats still enjoy games with their owners.

A kitten's sharp claws can get it into trouble.

This brave kitten is exploring up a ladder. ▷

Cat talk

Kittens can purr as loudly as a big cat when they are petted and stroked. They soon learn to weave affectionately around their owner's legs when they want food. Adult cats pull back their ears and arch their backs at their enemies. It is amusing to watch even very small kittens behaving in just the same way when they play fighting games together.

Kittens respond to human affection.

Six-week-old brothers play-fighting ▷

Growing up

A kitten usually starts life in a new home at about seven or eight weeks of age. It still needs frequent meals, plenty of milk and lots of sleep. By the time it is six months old it only needs two meals a day. The young cat reaches its full size when it is about eight months old. Cats can live for 15 or even 20 years.

This young cat is learning to hunt for itself.

This kitten is housebroken now and old enough to go to a new home. ▷